TROUT AND HOW TO CATCH THEM

TROUT AND HOW TO CATCH THEM

BY

P. CASTLE

EDINBURGH
OLIVER AND BOYD: TWEEDDALE COURT
1920

PREFACE

THE "tips" in this book should be valuable even to experienced trout fishers, and very much so to the fisherman who has got to the stage of casting a fair line with wet or dry fly, but who just misses making a basket when trout are down or not taking according to the book.

For instance, the method of fishing a lee shore of a loch, casting with the wind, is a very telling dodge not known to the generality of anglers

I consider that it is very good of Mr Castle to pass on his discoveries, for many highly skilled anglers rather incline to keep their particular methods secret. I have fished *per dies festos* for over fifty years—sticklebacks to whales—from back parts of China to the American continent, from the Arctic to the Antarctic. Owing to such experience the author has asked me to write this short preface, which I do with goodwill to the author and other anglers.

W G. BURN MURDOCH

March 1920

CONTENTS

vii

CONTENTS

TROUT AND HOW TO CATCH THEM

If you really want to hear and see Nature at its best, you should be on the banks of a stream at sunrise on a bright summer morning. You may have heard the birds' joyous song on a quiet summer evening, or after a thunderstorm, but to hear them at their very best this is the time.

When it comes mild at sunrise there is usually a good rise on; then is the time to put up a cast of small spiders, or a small worm, and you will get great sport casting up-stream over rising fish.

Fly Fishing

This is by far the most artistic mode of catching trout (though the floating worm, of which more anon, is quite close up). To learn how to make a cast, practise on a lawn, but for detailed instructions see a later chapter. There are various styles and casts, such as the Speyside, etc. There, even to expert fishers I must make one remark on the actual technique of fishing with fly, as it is a point that is not usually observed by fishers to whom those lines are addressed, and this is *to tie your flies :—*

The Correct Way

The Wrong Way.

Your dropper flies should always hang straight, not on back or side which is unnatural—the smallest fly to the point for the same reason one fishes a tapered cast.

Many anglers use a rod with a 2 or 3 lb. strain, and then fish-gut to hold 15 to 20 lb.   Now, apart from the fact that in all kinds of fishing the finer the tackle the more successful the angler, one × drawn gut and a good running reel will land anything up to 7 lb. weight if the fisher is at all expert.   That weight is well within what the trout angler may expect—in fact 2 lb. is usually a record trout in most waters—a great deal depends on the water you are fishing for length of cast.   Generally a three-yard cast is long enough, and, as I will explain later, two flies are best.   Two × drawn gut, in fact, is fine enough at all times, unless one

is fishing a very clear water with a bright sun.
It is only asking for trouble to use finer.
Keep out of sight and you will find two ×
drawn gut will not bother the trout.

Quite three parts of the fishing is keeping
out of sight, making the least possible disturb-

Finding the Far Bank at Night.

ance in the water—therefore fish up-stream all
the time and every time. You can thus use
a shorter line, and remember the shorter line
you can fish the more rises you can hook.
Get as low in the water as you can. On
approaching your pool, if you find you have
made a stumble or a clumsy approach, you
will find you lose nothing by kneeling stationary

for a minute or two before casting. Then cover the near water first at your side of river, gradually covering in a half circle to the opposite bank. The most likely place you will raise the big one of the pool is in the *shadow* of the far bank, which hides your gut more, and you can consequently deceive the trout better with all lures. It pays well, sometimes, if you have a good stretch of water to cover for the day, to fish only the shadow of the bank in each pool, of course keeping the sun in your face all the time.

Never fish lower than just opposite you. If you complete the half circle fishing upstream, you will cover all the water that is necessary. If the trout are not on the rise at the natural fly, begin with a slightly sunk fly. If no success sink lower, keeping the point of the rod close to the water, but don't drag. Let the stream take your fly down naturally. On the least stoppage, strike and get your rod up, keeping your fish playing above you, after taking a step or two back. This step or two taken slowly back means all the difference in spoiling the pool for another fish, and comes quite natural with practice. Never let your fish down below you, or you at once give the trout a four-to-one-on chance of getting away. When you come to the slower running part of your pool, it often pays well to pull slower, well sunk ; then occasionally a fairly quick jerk, stop, and pull again. This will often attract a trout that is not very keen on feeding.

When fish are bang on the feed they are easy of approach, but when off the rise or feed, the least movement seems to alarm them at once. On some occasions I have killed trout close to my feet when wading.

Practice alone will tell the angler how near he can approach a fish without disturbing it. When you have got as near as you think safe, by crawling up to your feeding fish, make one or two casts in the air to judge your distance ; then throw as lightly as you can over him or one foot above him.

Soft-Feathered Flies

For many years, the writer fished nothing but hackle or spider flies, and still believes the spider, taken all round, kills the best trout. It is certainly the most natural looking compared with the winged fly, in the water, and if dressed from the soft feathers of small birds has a life-like appearance. For experiment, take a hard hackled fly, as supplied by many tackle makers, and dip it up and down in a clear glass of water.   Then try a soft hackled fly, and you will be astounded at the difference. The one works up and down like a piece of stick, while the other moves out and in like a living insect.

If you wish to see how your fly appears to the trout, procure a small round piece of looking-glass—you can get one for about one penny from nearest toy shop (a boy's "shiner" will do); place it in a bowl full of water, and work your fly over it.   This will at once convince the angler of the superiority of soft-feathered flies.

Another Mode with Wet Fly

The following way will be found very deadly, and is known to very few anglers.   When one can fish long pools, use spiders or small-winged flies.   Cast a longish line, say a yard or thereby, above you, and let your flies sail until they are a yard below the horizontal; then commence to give short pulls about a foot each time, until the flies are nearly straight below you.   Pull and stop each time.   This method is very deadly in spring, and will kill

fish when they won't look at the fly fished in
the ordinary way.   It is the lively movement
of the flies that seem to tempt the trout.
The writer has proved this style to be very
successful on the Tweed.

Incident on Rosebery Loch

My friend P. and self struck a day when
there came quite a cloud of blue duns.   We
killed fish about while the hatch-out lasted.
After I put on two blue hen spiders (dressing—
the under-wing soft feather of the water-hen
summer plumage) and kept killing fish with
the sunk spider, my friend P. never got
another trout.   Now I hold that as long as
the trout were feeding on top the winged
flies deceived them , but when the trout went
down, my sunk spiders being more natural-
looking, kept deceiving and killing them.

Trout are more plentiful on sand or gravel
than on mud, where both exist on the pools
of your river ; generally pass over the sluggish,
deep pools and thin flats during daytime , the
latter are excellent for night fishing, but no
use during daytime.   Fish the streams and
rough waters, also close to banks where a fair
stream runs.   If fishing from the bank, go
warily without any stamping or moving

clumsily, as any vibration on the bank alarms the trout at once. In quiet streams, the fish feed more regularly and at stated intervals, and they seem to rest more regularly after a rise than on rapid running waters.

The capriciousness of trout as to rising is most extraordinary; many a time my friends and self have said on reaching the water, "Well, this day is made to order; we could not have ordered the conditions better," but for some unaccountable reason, there was not a move on. Then after fishing hours on end with little or no success, the trout all at once come on to take, though no hatch of flies has taken place meantime. On making inquiry, the other anglers fishing miles apart have the same tale to tell, and you will invariably find that the take came on exactly at the same time all over the river. This has often occurred on cold and wet days, as well as bright days, without any apparent change in the atmosphere, but some subtle change in the climatic conditions must surely be the cause; probably the clouds, with a change that is invisible to us poor mortals. The angler who discovers the cause and reason will have found the greatest of all angling secrets.

How Fish will take in a Gale

My friends A. and H., both excellent anglers, and self arrived one day on Rosebery Loch when it blew a gale. I took the weather shore, fishing spiders in the teeth of the wind. Fishing off the shore, killing trout in the lashed-up foam within two feet of the side, I got an excellent basket before 2 P.M. Fishing round the top end of loch by five o'clock I joined my friends who had fished the lee shore with the wind all day. I was surprised to find they had only one or two fish, whereas I had nineteen good trout. This proves that fish feed in a gale of wind on the drowned flies at weather side of loch. I had similar experience on Loch Achanalt in Ross-shire many years ago, and since have noticed the same on Loch Leven on a rough day.

The best fish hold the best feeding-ground. Where you kill a good trout, you will find on next visit another good one has taken up the same feeding place, as the big trout always secures the best feeding-ground, driving away his weaker brethren.

I am of opinion we fish far too many kinds of flies. I find in early spring on Border rivers, during March and April at least, if

B

you have a Greenwell, March brown, and a hare-lug, you need never change; for if you don't kill with those three they will take nothing.

For dry fly, Greenwell and blue upright is all you need, and that only from 10.30 till 2 in March, when the rise is usually on. In April, if the weather is mild, a rise may start about 11 till 3 P.M. After the rise, if it comes a cold, hard wind, you can go home for all the good you will do at this early season.

DRESSING FOR

Greenwell—

    B. Yellow tying silk waxed, and gold twist.

    W. Hen blackbird wing.

    H. Black red

March Brown—

    B. Hare's ear with gold tinsel.

    W. Pheasant tail, single wing.

    H. Dark partridge.

March Brown (spider preferred)—

    B. Hare's ear, gold top.

    H. Dark partridge.

Hare-lug—

    B. ⎱ Pick out with needle to form hackle.
    H. ⎰

    W Single, inside of woodcock wing.

From April to end of May, Greenwell, March brown, with flat all-gold body. Sam

Slick and partridge spider with yellow body is all that is required. Rise usually on from 11 till 3 towards end of May if mild weather, in the evening from 5 to 7.

Sam Slick—
- B. Hare-lug, gold tip flat, and gold tinsel
- W. Hen pheasant.
- H Rather light partridge.

Partridge Spider—
- B. Yellow silk.
- H. Dark to light partridge, soft feather.

When fish are not rising to the natural fly, and consequently not on the surface of the water, a sunk fly with a slow jerky movement will often give surprising results. This only applies to brown trout. When sea trout are off, nothing you may try seems to tempt them. Never miss the hang of the stream, as good fish usually lie there. The hang is the smooth water at the end of a pool, and flowing quickly to the top of the next rough water. When a strong gale is blowing, you will find good trout take well just above where the stream breaks.

Sunk Fly.

Often when a big hatch of flies are on, fish don't take the artificial fly well. Try a pool where you find only occasional natural flies, and you will invariably get a rise. After the big hatch is over, fish up the rough streams with a sunk fly, and try to avoid fishing with the sun on your back.

Horse-hair is much preferable to gut for fine fishing. The advantages are, there is no splash, and it does not shine in the water like gut. One disadvantage is, that it is very apt to get into tangles and requires an expert to fish it. Many of the good Clyde anglers fish nothing else, using six and eight flies on a cast, and landing trout up to 2 lb. weight.

The throwing of your fly or bait, even if badly executed, will often not alarm the trout; but let him get even a shadow of you and he is at once wary. Remember his sense of sight is most acute.

Use two flies only. I used to fish three or four, but, when night fishing, I found the great advantage in fishing two, and later on found I could do just as well with same number in daytime.

Though I dressed my own flies, using mostly spiders during day, I dressed them to please myself, and I believe, also, the trout. I never got any great praise for my efforts in this line from brother anglers, so I don't intend or pretend to give any lessons on fly-dressing.

I may say I found I could kill even better
with a rough-dressed fly of right colour and
soft feathers than with shop specimens. These,
in my humble opinion, have too much on them.
With winged flies I find a single wing did
better than two.

Fishing Down-stream

If you must fish in this way, take the best
cover you can, behind bushes, etc., to
approach or crawl along flat near enough to
work, then cast rather above you and work
your flies without any drag. When one place
has been fished, repeat your tactics farther
down. If bright weather, you will find it pay
you to rest a few minutes after getting into
position before you commence casting. This
gives any trout you may have disturbed a
chance to settle again.

If there is a high bank, rather wade along-
side if possible, as your shadow may be thrown
many yards from the top of the bank, and
you are seen easily. But if you move quietly,
with no splashing, the trout have less chance
of seeing you if the bank is your background.
Pass long, sluggish pools and thin flats during
day fishing, unless you can cast over a rising

fish in a strong breeze. You will find your time better employed fishing the streams.

I have observed for many years in all streams that after the first week in August fly fishing is poor. Trout do not rise well again until September. The only reason I can assign for this is, that the trout have got surfeited with the fly harvest of June and July, and are now getting so much bottom feeding with the fresh-water snail (then at its best) that they go off fly diet for a time.

Rising Short

In stream fishing, there is no one so quick in striking as the trout is in taking your fly. Very often rising short is blamed when it is the angler who is too slow on the strike. When trout are not feeding keenly, no doubt they sometimes come at the fly in a half-hearted manner, often with no intention of taking it; but when bang on the feed, they mean business every time. Then the angler cannot be too quick in striking, as the rise he sees is generally the turn of the fish taking down the fly.

In certain lights an optical delusion occurs so far as the trout is concerned, as the effect

of the light is apt to show the fly at a
greater or less distance than it really is. This
is one of the principal causes of so-called
rising short. If you are missing many fish, it
is a good plan to shorten your line.

A Rough Stream River

One can often do well fishing a large spider
in the roughest of the water, casting often,
with a short line just about length of your
rod. Keep a steady strain on but no drag,
and strike on the least stoppage. When you
find your small flies not doing, the big spider
often makes a good basket.

Eyed flies are certainly more economical,
but after fishing them for many
years I completely discarded them,
because they never hang well, nor
look nearly so natural as the gut-tied
specimens.

When rivers get very low in June or July,
if you do not fish the small up-stream worm,
try very small spiders sunk.

Black Spider—

> B. Brown silk and quill body mixed.
> H. Cock starling; a dot of peacock herl at
> top may be added with advantage.

Plover Spider—

    B. Yellow silk, with flat gold tip.

    H. Golden plover.

Snipe Blae—

    B. Straw silk.

    H. Inside snipe's wing.

Tomtit*—

    B. Slate and orange silk mixed.

    H. Tomtit's tail feather very sparsely dressed.

Were it not that one misses a lot of fish, after being hooked, through the slight hold, I should never fish any larger than 12's or 13's during day in river fly fishing.

Other Lures

In the writer's opinion, we fish far too much with the one lure for trout. Better baskets can be got with equally good sport, just as artistically as, say, with fly, with slugs, creepers, grub, natural fly, beetles, etc., in fact with all insects trout feed on. Fish either like a dry fly or a sunk fly on fine tackle. I maintain that trout will take the above lures more freely and with less suspicion than the artificial fly, with which they get pricked so frequently during the season.

* This is a very deadly fly in small water.

In most of our hard fished rivers and lochs, the trout are so well educated to artificial flies, that they can almost tell who dressed them. I will endeavour to explain how several of these lures can be fished with success.

Natural Fly

Daddy - long - legs, May fly, alder fly, wood fly (found on horse manure), grasshoppers, bluebottle, etc., all are deadly, fished with a fine line in a good breeze. This is called dapping : Bait one or two flies through the back just below the head joint ; on a No. 2 hook at the end of a tapered gut cast, three yards in length, and allow the breeze to carry out the line ; keep dancing the fly on top of water, and if there is a strong breeze blowing, the fly will work quite naturally ; but if the breeze is light the angler requires to work the fly.

Cow Dung Beetle

This is perhaps one of the most deadly natural baits, especially in Cow Dung Beetle. sluggish streams, a lure you will find is very seldom fished. The beetle is found

c

in cow dung two to four days old, usually beneath but also in the dung. They keep alive for days if placed in a tin with perforated lid and a little moss. Use a No. 1, flat-hammered hook preferred, and in baiting pass the hook at the head joint and just above the wings and bring it out at the bottom of the belly; a tapered two to three yard gut cast, with a fairly pliable tippy rod, cast well under shadowy bushes and banks; sink it, but with no lead used, and strike on the least stoppage.

To be thoroughly successful with this style of fishing, you must be prepared to crawl about, keeping well out of sight. Many anglers soon get tired after trying one or two likely places, but, if you persevere, you often find on a poor day, when others are doing next to nothing with fly or worm, that you are the only one killing fish. Even on an average day, when all lures are killing a few trout, on comparison at night you will generally find that your basket is heaviest, though perhaps with only half the number of trout.

There is another beetle, found on the under web of ferns, which can be used in the same way, but I much prefer the cow dung specimen.

Don't use the larger red-bellied ones, as they are too soft in the water. You can also fish the beetle by trans-fixing from head to tail, raising the wings. If you fish two, pass the first right up the hook.

Fern Beetle.

Cow Dung Beetle. (Raised wing.)

Wasp Grub

Add a little salt to a pot of boiling water, and put your grubs in for two or three minutes. While boiling strain off, and dry on top of stove or oven. Fish one or two on a flat-hammered hook, say No. 2. Does well on a close, sultry night when fly not taking. Fish sunk without leads, same as beetle.

Wasp Grub.

Caddis or Stick-bait

Found at bottom under stones in running water and near the sides. The stick you will find about one inch long, covered with fine sand and very small stones. You will see the black head of the grub, after breaking the top of stick. Pull out the grub by the head, and fish it as above, using a smaller hook.

Caddis or Stick-bait.

Docken Grub

Found in the roots of dockens and in the roots of tansy—a most deadly bait. Transfix the grub from head to tail on a No. 3 or 4 hook, fine wire. When the fish strike, you will often find the grub shot up the cast, and it can be used again. Fish same as worm—no lead; often good at night or after a flood when nothing else will take.

Docken Grub.

Creeper or Stone Fly

Found under the stones in clear running water from end of April and during May, and

Creeper.   Catching Creepers.   Creeper Hook.

is about $1\frac{1}{2}$ inches long. Best way to catch them is to use a small muslin net. Raise the stone up towards the stream, holding your net close to below the stone. Of course you can get them with your hands, but the net is much quicker. Keep in a tin with some wet moss. Fish it with two hooks, about $\frac{3}{4}$ inch

apart—the top hook say a No. 2, the bottom
a No. 1   Bait the creeper with the larger
top hook just under the joint at neck, right
through with point obtruding over the barb,
the end hook through the tail end of creeper.
Fish it up-stream, with or without a small lead
only in the rough water.   Strike whenever it
stops.   If very rough water, one or two small
split shot may be used about one foot from
the bait.   A bright day with clear sun will be
found best.   The largest and best-conditioned
trout are taken by creeper, which only lasts
about six weeks.   On the Whitadder it does
not do well below Chirnside, the reason being,
perhaps, that you don't get creepers lower
down than Chirnside Mill.   It is a very deadly
bait on all streams during May and June.
The creeper's next stage is the stone fly which
you can collect, wherever creepers are found,
under stones at side of river and crawling on
the banks   It can be fished for another month
in same manner with similar hooks, but no
lead used.

May Fly

The Bobbing Minnow

This is a very pleasing way of catching trout, which is not much exercised. It is best fished during May and June on very bright days with a small water—the sun cannot be too bright. After first week in July I have never found it do well. The only reason I can assign for this is, that the live minnow apparently only acts like the bobbing minnow during these months.

It is strange the Tweed never fishes well with this mode of angling, although some parts of this grand river one would think

Bobbing Minnow.

were made to order for it.

Freshly caught minnows are best about $1\frac{1}{2}$ inches long, the beardies doing just about as well as the ordinary. If these are not easily obtained, use the salted minnow.

How to Salt Minnows

Place in layers freshly killed minnows in a flat tin box with rough kitchen salt, mixed with just a little saltpetre. Place the minnows in as dry as possible, and pour off the water that will form on them, adding more salt from

time to time until no more water will run off.
Don't put in very baggy ones as the belly
usually bursts first pull.

Best fished on a single hook, say No. 5 or 6,
fine-wired, flat-hammered preferred, as it is
much sharper.   A hollow lead about $\frac{1}{4}$ ounce
is placed on the hook.   Procure a needle three
inches long with a thin eye—a darning needle
will do with the eye cut (a delicate job to cut
them).   Thread your needle from mouth of
the minnow right through
the body and out at the
vent.   Having put your gut
through the broken eye of
your needle, pull through

Bobbing Minnow.

until the lead is in body of the minnow, the
hook then being across the mouth.   Tie your
gut with piece of fine thread close to the tail.
This prevents your minnow from doubling
up, and is more natural-looking.   A small
swivel half way up your two-yard cast of 1 x gut
gives the minnow an extra turn each pull up
and down.   Fish it by bobbing up and down
with fairly slow one-yard pulls, behind and
between bushes, at sides of steep rocky pools.
Keep bobbing at all depths for some time at
each place, keeping well out of sight.   In fact,
only the point of a short rod should be over

the bank or rock you work at.   You can easily
get to know the rate to pull up and down
according to your weight of lead by watching
your minnow work for a time.   If it goes down
too quickly and not with zigzag plunges, lighten
your lead by scraping it with your knife until

Thin Lead
Pipe.

Bobbing for Trout

you get the right weight to zigzag properly
with the size of minnows you are using.   You
may soon become expert and be able to work it
in two feet of water.   If you feel a slight strain
and then a slack, the trout has been there but
not held.   Still keep working till you feel he
has hold, then give him a second or two to
gorge it, and strike firm.   Work with your
right hand, keeping a yard or two of slack
line in your left, to ease quickly when you feel
a fish.   Sometimes you will find a trout just
nosing the minnow, sailing round it and hitting
it with his nose, not offering to mouth it.
After bobbing a bit with such a non-feeder,
give a quick jerk to the side.   He then thinks
he is going to lose it, and often makes a bold

grab and you have him on.   The deep rocky
pools above Elba on the Whitadder is the
finest bit of water I have ever fished at this
game.

One gets the largest trout, and cannibal
trout, that will take no other lure, often fall a
victim to the bobbing or plouting minnow.   An
Ayton angler killed an old trout over 6 lb.
at Elba in 1917, and that after being broken
with him an hour previously.   It does well
in some lochs on a calm, bright day, in deep
parts near weeds.   Anchor your boat a length
or two outside the bank of weeds.   After your
boat has settled down quite still, start bobbing
at bow or stern with a 12- to 14-foot rod.
The trout lying in the weeds dart out at your
bait, grand sport being got at times with the
big fellows.

When at night fly fishing and you want a
rest for half an hour, if you get on a clean
shingle or sandy bottom and take the trouble
to put on the minnow baited as for bobbing,
leave it lying on the bottom.   You can often
get a big trout in this way.   It does not
necessarily need to be a deep part.   In the
calm water at side of the current at top end
of pool, where the large trout come to feed
at night, you will invariably get a good fish.

Let him gorge it, and you will hear your reel sing when he is there. Some anglers will say this is not a very sporting way to get them, but it passes the time profitably whilst you are resting, when out for a good basket. You will find eels bother you on mild nights as they take the minnow greedily, but on frosty nights, when the minnow usually does well, you won't be troubled with the eel. On such nights he goes into the mud. I find the best way to bait is to cut your gut each time you put on a fresh minnow about eighteen inches from the hook. Some use a watchmaker's spring at the swivel, which does away with cutting gut each time, but I find this is more clumsy and more likely to frighten the fish.

The Charm of Night Fishing

From May to the end of the trouting season, for a great many years back, the writer has fished mostly at night, for several reasons, viz., one gets the best and largest trout at night; you have not nearly such hard work as in day fishing, as one does not need to move about so much—in fact a couple of good pools is quite enough for a good night's fishing.

If you do not know your water and the

pools where quantity of trout lie, come down
to your river an hour or so before dusk.
Stroll quietly along the bank till you see two

Do Trout take by Moonlight?

likely-looking pools, or where you see a good
move of fish.   Take a rest till you see the
evening rise on, and fish your small
flies till it gets dark.   Then put on
your night cast of two flies (more
than two only get you into tangles
and messes in the dark), Nos. 2 or
3 if no moon, but if bright moon,
No. 1 size will be large enough.
If the moon is up, it is equally
necessary to fish up as during the day, but fish
very slowly, making as little movement in the

water as possible.   Start at bottom of the thin
flats, moving a yard or two at a time, then
keep casting above and completing a half circle
till you have covered the water several times.
Move another yard or two and repeat; each
stand should be at least fifteen minutes.   Continue right up to the neck of the pool, and if
the two pools you have selected are about 300
yards in all, that is quite sufficient ground for
the night.

If the night is dark, you can fish down
provided you move very slowly, making no
splashing; just shuffle along a few inches at a
time, and fish stationary for fifteen minutes or
more at each fresh stand.

You have longer time to each cast fishing
down, as I will explain.   In night fishing
down-stream you act in very much different
way from the day style, when you never let
your flies come further below you than to the
horizontal.   Start by casting well up as near
the far bank as possible, and follow your
sinking flies till your line is right below you,
without much of a drag however.   If no offer
up till then, give your line one or two gentle
bobs up and down by raising and lowering the
point of your rod.   If still no offer, draw slowly
up until your rod is half perpendicular, and

make your next cast. You will find you will often get a trout after your cast has spent with either the bobbing or the slow draw. This is especially so fishing the most deadly of all night lures, the beef maggot, of which more anon.

In night fishing, don't move much about, for if you do you are only spoiling good water. You have a much better chance of making a good basket if fishing very slowly as described, than roving over many pools and much ground at night. A good plan is to try find the far bank, letting your tail-fly actually land on grass or sedges, then pull it gently off. The best fish lie at night close to the bank, waiting the flies falling off the grass or sedges. Once the angler has fished a river a few times, he will find from experience he can fish within a few inches of the far bank without hooking and tangling. On wet nights any feeding fish move in mid-water ; there being no flies on the sedges or rushes, the trout don't lie near the banks. In addition to a mild, balmy night, a good sign is to see the bats coming out at dusk, a sure sign of night flies on the move. On a real good night, you will find the night flies crawling on your coat and cap and on to your neck (many a trout the writer has killed baiting the living fly on end of his hook, throwing the cast lightly and letting it swim slowly down).

If the east haar rises on the water about dusk, generally you can look out for a cold and bad fishing night. Rainy nights often fish well, and very cold nights without fog do well at times.

When the rivers get stagnant through want of rain in July and August, trout don't take well. At the same time I believe you can't get too small waters for night fishing. April even fishes well at night, if the nights are fairly mild; but strange to say, I have killed some of my best baskets with fly in April and September when cold nights prevailed. One night in particular I got a 12-lb. basket of brown trout on the Whitadder, my fingers being so benumbed with the frost that I lost several good trout taking off the hook after netting them.

In the months from May to August, the following are all the flies necessary, size No. 1 or 2 according to light :—

March Brown, with gold tinsel.

March Brown Spider, with gold body (flat).

Woodcock, Yellow, with gold or silver tip.

A Spider Fly, dressed thus: Mixed hackles, say peacock herl, and black red, on the top of flat gold body,

and a *Greenwell*.

After first ten days of August you can begin to fish with

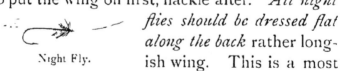

Mixed Spider Fly.

Alexandria—

    B. Flat silver (no tinsel).

    H. Sheeny black.

    W. Peacock with golden pheasant crest on back

Mallard—

    B. Flat gold (no tinsel)

    H. Yellow red.

    W. Darkish mallard wing.

Pheasant Back—

    B. Flat gold.

    H. Red.

    W. Pheasant back, mottled feather.

Bustard—

    B. Gold or silver, flat

    H Light partridge.

    W. Light bustard with black speck.

These you will find all that is necessary.

N.B.—In dressing night flies, I find it best to put the wing on first, hackle after. *All night flies should be dressed flat along the back* rather long-ish wing. This is a most important point, as you will find all night flies' wings lie flat along the back. Only some

Night Fly.

small midges are cocked like the majority of day flies. On hot nights, if the fly is not killing well, try the natural minnow. On the

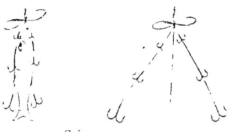

Spinners.

shallows, the best spinner I found was a Stewart tackle spinner, head made of amber-coloured celluloid, with fine wire to transfix the body. I used to get the old-fashioned watch-cases to make the head or gills—the other rather wobbles than spins but does equally well.

Dry Fly at Night

One might think that dry fly would not be much good at night, but I found a large dry

Dry Flies.

fly, No. 2, does well on warm nights, when trout are on the surface feeding on the large night flies. The first time I was successful with dry fly at night was on the pool above the railway bridge at Cardrona-on-Tweed. I had fished carefully down the red gates pools and next flat, but had not killed a trout after the evening rise from 8.30 P.M. till 1 A.M. Still the trout were plopping about here and there until I came to the bend with the dense wood on the right bank. Here the trout were rising like mad, close under the trees. A cloudy moon was on, so I tried the usual flies, teal and red and bracken clock among the rising fish for the best part of an hour, only getting one pull. I came ashore at my usual time, about two, for a sandwich and a smoke. Still the trout kept plump, plop. I had some No. 2 dry flies I dressed specially to try on a loch (where I had no success with them), putting on a blae and silver flat body. Second cast I was into a good one. I kept casting where I thought the rise was, and got fifteen beauties, one over $1\frac{1}{2}$ lb., in about an hour and a half. Several times since then I have fished dry fly at night with success, especially on the Tweed, Tyne, and Whitadder. Now one would think trout could not distinguish colour at night, but I had a peculiar experience, I think worth while relating, at Elba on the Whitadder one night in September. I had a No. 1 pheasant

E

back and yellow on my bob fly, and kept taking every trout on it. After a time I changed my tail fly to a woodcock and yellow (being nearest I had in No. 1 to pheasant back). Still the bob kept getting all my fish. I again changed the bob to the tail with same result, every fish on the pheasant back.

Now there is not much difference to look at a dark woodcock and pheasant back, both having same colour of body; but seemingly the trout could tell. Had I not changed the position of the fly, I would have said the bob fly was working more naturally. I wonder could Sir Herbert Maxwell explain the foregoing, after his theory of colour-sense in fish?

I find on clear moonlight nights the larger flies keep to the banks and do not get on the water as on dark nights. This provides another reason for using nothing larger than No. 1, or even day river size on clear nights.

When there is a heavy dew, or on starry nights with frost, the minnow does well. You can spin it much more slowly than during daytime, and fish a shorter line. But the most deadly form of night fishing is with the beef maggot, to which I shall devote a special chapter.

I have often found a very rough night do

specially well on the lower reaches of the Tweed, say from Twizell to three miles below Norham Bridge.

If you are fishing a bank where horses are grazing, you need not be alarmed if they show preference for your company. The horse likes to be near mankind and will often follow the angler about at night.

On the banks of the long dam, about a quarter mile below Hutton Bridge on the Whitadder, where I have had many glorious nights, were for many years two old pensioners, a horse and donkey belonging to my friend Mr Milne, the farmer. While I fished, slowly wading, they used to follow along the bank for hours. So tame did the donkey get that on calling him he used to share my sandwich about two in the morning, though I never could get the old horse to come to my hand. What with the owls in the woods on the far bank, and these two dumb friends, I never felt lonely though I seldom or never met a soul from 8 P.M. till 5 A.M., when I usually finished.

Maggot Fishing

This is to my idea the most deadly mode of angling for trout, because it is life and so attractive. No other lure you may try keeps so long alive, nor has the same lively movement. Much practice is required to make an expert maggot fisher. The angler must have a very acute sense of touch, in fact he must be able to feel the least touch on the line, as often the trout taking the sunk, slowly-moving fly and

maggot only make a tremble on the line as he sucks in the wriggling maggot. On your fly landing near the far bank, before it has had time

Night Fly, with Maggot.

to sink, he will often go bang at it. Then the angler finds the need of an easy-running reel, or a break is the inevitable result.

The maggot is fished on the ordinary night fly by putting the point of the hook over the barb, through the thick or tail end of the maggot, allowing the head part to wriggle about, which makes your fly so natural and attractive to the trout. It does equally well with sea trout, and is fished very slowly, sunk fly as before mentioned. In night fishing, first find your far bank and cast as close as possible to it. Cast well up above you, and draw very slowly until you find your line right below you. Should you not get a pull or touch up till then, move your rod gently up and down two or three times as you see salmon fishers work their fly, against the stream at end of cast, then slowly draw your flies up till your rod is half perpendicular, or far enough up so that you can make your next cast easy. You have not the same chance of hooking your fish as when you are slowly sailing sunk across the water (often very near the bottom), but some nights you will find the bobbing and drawing-up method at end of your cast is the way you will kill most of your basket.

The shorter line you can fish applies here same as day fishing, and the more certain are you of your trout. Strike on the least stoppage, then get your fish as quickly as possible above you.

The angler will find trout are much easier to kill at night than during day, as they seem not to have the same fear as when they see one well. A good trout will often come sliding to the net after his first run, if you keep his head just out of the water; but should you miss him and he sees you, he may give you a busy few minutes till you tire him out.

I intend later to devote a special line or two regarding the netting of your fish—one or two flies, never more at night; where there are many weed banks you will do best using one only, and not many varieties.   In maggot fishing, trout often come boldly a second time after your fresh maggot, even when you think they must have felt the hook.

After day breaks the maggot is of little use, but it can be fished later on in the day, and is often very deadly, using a showy fly, quick casting up rough water.   Do not miss even the very roughest parts in the neck of the stream.   You can then use a line about length of your rod, and let the stream take your fly down naturally and with no drag, and strike on least stoppage.   A good one × gut cast is necessary here, as you must strike

Day Maggot Fishing.   Maggot for Bottom Fishing.

quick and strong.   Another way during day is to use, say, a No. 13 bare hook, bait one maggot right up the hook, and another as before, leaving the body wriggling.   On one occasion I killed a good basket of herling on the Fleet at Gatehouse, on a very bright day and a fine water, fishing in this manner.

Where you have a clean bottom, it can also be used with a No. 2 bare hook, baiting three or four maggots through the thick part, drawing very slowly over the bottom. This way is most deadly at night, if you are sure of a sandy or small pebble bottom.

The following flies are enough for maggot fishing :—

> *March Brown*—With gold tip and body of gold twist on hare-lug.
>
> *March Brown*—Hackle fly.
>
> *Woodcock*— Gold body, black red or red H.
>
> *Light Mallard*—Wing, peacock herl body, black hackle Use Nos 1, 2, or 3 according to the moon, from May to August
>
> .After August has come in—
> *Teal and Silver*—Black hackle.
>
> *Alexandria*—
>> B Plain silver.
>> W. Peacock and golden pheasant crest.
>> H. Magenta.
>
> *Teal and Gold*—Black hackle, plain gold flat
>
> *Greenwell*—On moonlight nights.
>
> *Golden Plover*—Hackle, gold body, for both brown and sea trout
>
> *Light Bustard* and flat gold. Yellow or red hackle
>
> *Pheasant Buck*—Yellow (darkish) gold tip, light partridge hackle (this is excellent fly in September)
>
> *Teal and Bustard* will be found good for sea trout

How to Keep Maggots.

During hot weather keep maggots in small tin boxes with bran, which hardens and whitens them, but not too deep in bran. A drop or two of ammonia keeps them cool. Bury them a foot deep in shade, and take up one box as required. Best maggots are got from skin works, but any butcher can supply them in hot weather from his bone box, or you can get them by post from the breeders in England.

Loch Fishing

Fishing a loch from a boat is far removed from the real thing in angling, and the fishers who have only angled in this way (and there are many of them) are somewhat surprised when you tell them they know very little about angling. The French idiom "Vous savez tout, sauf, ce qu'il faut savoir" comes very appropriate here.

There is certainly skill in loch fishing, but not one-tenth the skill required for river fishing. The average good angler would much rather fish a Highland burn. A good river fisher will always make a good loch fisher, but on the other hand the loch fisher has to learn over again, and is simply lost when he comes to match his wits against the wily river trout. Give a good river fisher a loch he can readily wade from the shore, and you can back him every time against the loch fisher with boat.

In moorland or dark-coloured lochs, fancy flies, reds with tinsel bodies, will invariably be found to kill. In clear-water lochs, quiet colours do best.

The less motion you make with the boat, and the lower you can get yourself on the water, the better chance you have. Never stand up while casting ; for example, while wading a loch, see how far your waves of motion are carried on a smooth water. This is the trouts' telegraph for danger!

All flies should be worked partly with the wind, not dead against it as most anglers do. If the wind is strong, cast sideways into it, drawing slowly partly across the wave. If the breeze is light, you can cast well up the wind from either end of boat. This you will find is one of the greatest successes in loch fishing, and you can see that the flies work more naturally. You cannot strike quickly enough in loch fishing, as nineteen times out of twenty

F

the rise you see is the fish turning with your fly. Ask yourself how many fish you kill in the season with a surface fly; why, when you cast over a rising fish, you are surest of it when you dwell a second after the cast; this is so that your fly may sink somewhat. Watch your best anglers on, say, Loch Leven; see how slowly they pull, and they all fish a sunk fly. Many of those anglers will be astonished to hear they often fish a fly sunk half a foot and more. The majority of the natural loch flies hatch in the water, therefore the fish feed mostly on them when they are rising to the surface. Never miss a streak of foam, and cast in front of rushes or bank of weeds; the best trout usually lie there.

Rough Spider.

On a very rough day, take the shore at tail-end of wind (the weather shore); there you will find the trout feeding on the drowned flies, in the very roughest of broken water and foam, and very close into the shore. Spiders are usually best of a good size.

The average loch fly has far too much dressing; get your flies tied with about half the usual amount and dressed with soft feathers Work them slowly, sunk; this especially applies to a rough day when the gale and movement of your boat gives a natural motion to the fly under water. If the trout are not rising, fish the shallow water, as you may tempt a trout to come up there, whereas if the water is deep you have much less chance.

If you see a fish following your tail fly, work more quickly with a slight jerky movement, and he will often come bang at it and take. If you are fishing across the wave, try your bob fly just tipping the water; this you will find deadly with a strong breeze.

Where you are staying for a time on your loch, take the temperature of the water on a day the trout are doing well; you will find the loch will again fish well when you have the same or warmer temperature.

Floating Worm Fishing on Lochs

Very few anglers know how this can be done, and to many of them this mode will appear at first sight nothing short of poaching. But fishing a worm like a sunk fly requires as much or more skill than ordinary fly fishing; it is equally as skilful and

Baiting Worm.

sometimes it is more deadly. Some use a tapered cast with two hooks about one inch apart; bait a good-sized worm, leaving a long tail; put your barb right through the worm half inch below the head, the other hook through a good inch from the tail, and use no lead. Others much prefer a single hook. Cast a fairly

Fishing a Weather Shore.

long line, and draw and sink alternately, slowly, and don't be too quick to strike. Do not miss fishing near banks of weed or large stones.

I know an angler who has been very successful with the worm in loch fishing. He stalks the rise : this is done more easily with two in the boat, the rower backing to within casting distance of the place he saw a rise. Then chopping the boat, the fisher in the stern,

standing with a long rod and line, casts the
worm on the rise or slightly on the weather
side.   There is no sinker used; the worm
slowly sinks and often is taken with a dash
and often let go so quickly the angler has no
time to strike.   The idea is to have slack line
in hand ready to let go, if it continues running
strike; if it stops, the worm has been dropped.
Do not then pull in, but leave the worm sinking
and the trout will come to it again.   You will
then be ready to strike whilst the line is
moving away.

Fishing a Calm

Fish spiders, casting a long line out from
bow or stern of boat, and let your flies sink
well and draw slowly.   Row your boat slowly,
and after a stroke or two let her glide along
Often you will do well with spent gnats dressed
flat.   I never yet found a loch where dry

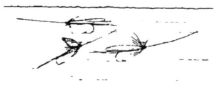

Sunk Flies.

fly did really well, but have killed trout
during day with a small maggot on the spent
gnat.   Trolling minnow on a loch is not

angling, but if you must fish it use a rather pliable rod ; don't grip your rod immediately a fish strikes, for it will hook itself if left a second or so after striking, but with a stiff pointed rod you will miss one out of three pulls.

Worm Fishing

During the months of June and July, when the streams are very low, then is the time for some real sport—fishing up with the small worm. You must fish fine, never missing a bit of water, behind stones or in small runs with only an inch or two of water—for at this time trout lie in the most unlikely places. Fish two hooks, with a small pink worm preferred, as a rule without leads. Most of your fish in the streams will be found to take it like the fly. Worm Fishing. Strike quickly whenever you see your fish, as he is then turning with your worm. Another way is to fish a round bend, throwing a fairly long line just in front of weeds or in the shadow of the bank ; but in this mode, when your fish takes hold yield to him, and then strike. If you strike or pull when you feel a fish he will throw it from him on feeling least resistance.

Round Bend.

Sea Trout Fishing

Perseverance applies more so here than in brown trout fishing. Nothing seems to move sea trout until his feeding time comes, and I believe you cannot get too rough a day —in fact, a howling day with wind and rain seems to do best. I killed my record basket on Loch Strand, Shetland, in September 1912 (fifty-two sea trout with fly), when the wind was blowing a gale and the rain came down in sheets.

You will often fish all day and never get an offer or see a fish move, then get a good basket in two hours when they make a move. They don't seem to mind cold so much as yellow trout do, fishing best at the *moon's changes*. Whether day or night fishing, *full moon you will find best*. I am beginning to think the moon's changes also apply to brown trout, but have not proved it so conclusively as it is to sea trout.

Whether on river, voe, or loch, the most deadly fly for sea trout is the *garden fly*, i.e., a large black-headed worm—the bigger the better—fishing up-stream with a slow pull, and keep up the slow pull when he comes at your bait. When you feel a bold pull, strike hard.

Sea trout flies are usually gaudy and quite differently worked from brown trout fishing.  During the day they are best fished on top of water ; cast a fair line to their lie, then keep your rod well up with your flies dancing on the water. I find the sea trout comes with open mouth following your fly on top of water, whereas the brown trout comes up at your fly.

They take well at night, in fact best baskets are got on cloudy, moonlit nights, and do well with long winged night flies ; fished with or

Sea and Brown Trout Rising.

without the maggot as described in night fishing ; fished in the same manner, with exception that you don't need to move about, even so much as in brown trout fishing, once you find the various feeding places on either river or loch. Sea trout seem to have special lies where they will be found season after season. Once you discover these, you need not waste time moving about much, as the fish run in shoals. You may get a busy fifteen to twenty minutes at a place, and then have to wait there as long for the next run, without an offer. When fishing tidal waters, the first three hours of the flood and first two of the ebb are best.

It is not generally known that under the red tangle on sea coast you can put in some hard work getting a worm that is to be found at the roots. This bait is *simply irresistible* to sea trout.

The following flies are enough to use either night or day, sizes according to weather conditions—never larger than No. 3 :—

Castle Kergood—

    B Flat, silver or gold.
    Tip. Red crow.
    H. Sheeny black.
    W. Peacock, with two strands golden pheasant
       crest on outside.
    Cheeks. Two small Jungle cock

Teal and Turkey mixed—

    B. Mohair yellow and red.
    W. Mixed turkey and teal ; mandarin drake
       best.
    H Black sheeny.

G

Claret and Silver—

    B. Plain silver body and claret.

    W. Mallard

    H. Claret.

Mixed Spider dressed—

    H. Peacock herl, black red, peacock herl

    B. Plain gold.

Turkey and Peacock—

    B. Half silver and peacock herl

    H. Black.

    W. Mandarin drake.

March Brown.

Sea trout take a large worm in voes or tidal waters; fished as before-mentioned on two hooks with a long tail left. Change your worm often, as the salt water soon kills it. No doubt the trout here take it for their natural food, the sand eel, which can be fished in the same manner. A small swivel half up your cast is an advantage, for it allows your bait an extra natural turn. Persevere with worm for it will kill at least three to one against fly.

Spring Sea Trout

It is my belief that the run of so-called spring fish are in the majority mended kelts, that is, fish that have spawned early, consequently early back to the sea, and have mended up. On the other hand one gets plump, well-filled fish in spring. These are grilse of the sea trout—fish that have not spawned. These fish, I maintain, are to be found all the season in the voes or estuaries. They no doubt come up to the fresh water and work about the brackish waters to get rid of their enemy the sea lice. *Yellow or orange fins* are a hybrid of yellow and sea trout.

Trout do not take well—

With a falling barometer ; before a storm ; south wind, hot day ; haze on hills ; hard wind, dry, bright sun ; dark windy days without rain ; leaden-coloured water ; when the fly is not on the water.

Feeding Spots

In every river and loch there are certain places where fish take more readily than others ; the reason is that there are various spots which are good feeding ground.

I will endeavour to explain where these places are to be found on both loch and river, giving a few examples I have proved on one or two pools on well-known waters. But once the angler knows his river, he will soon discover the best lies of the trout. A golden rule to follow is, wherever you get a good trout, say behind some stone, under a bush, or immediately in slack water at side of the current near an overhanging bank, on your return visit, even the following day, there you will find another good trout, as you have struck a good feeding place.

To prove this, during the spring of 1917, on the Whitadder, the writer often met an angler seemingly always on the run, in fact some of the regulars named him " The Fleeing Fisher," for he used to start a mile below Hutton Bridge between seven and eight in the morning, fish up to Edington Mill (about $4\frac{1}{2}$ miles of water), then fish back by about six P.M. If the trout were doing at all well, he had invariably a good basket of trout above the average weight. He was far from what one would call a good caster, though he had the knack of keeping out of sight, as many a time I have watched him crawling to get in position for covering a good lie. On one occasion I asked him why he covered so much water, and he explained that he just fished the places he had killed good trout in his twenty years' experience of fishing that water. I supplied him that day with one or two of my spiders that were doing well, and from that time he never passed me on the water without a word or two. Before then, the anglers said, he was never known to speak to anyone in his " fleeing " expeditions.

Special feeding places on loch and river apply equally as well to sea trout as to brown trout ; in fact, in tidal waters sea trout and herling take best in exactly the same places year after year. For example :—

River Fleet at Gatehouse.—Famed for its herling and sea trout, taking the three tidal pools above the Crag Pool, just round the bend, left bank going up from the Crag Pool ; there is an opening of about fifteen feet between the bushes. This is one of the best lies for both sea trout and herling on the river. The next lie going up the water is at the tail end of the " Tree Root " pool, well into the left bank under the trees ; further up about sixty yards a bend with a square green bank and deep water with tall grass at edge ; close in here is real good for a big one. Then continue up to the top of this pool, and cast into the bare open bit, just above the big tree on left bank. One hundred and fifty yards farther up you come to the " 4 Ash Pool " or " Strangers'

Pool," good from neck to deep part under overhanging bush on left bank. Coming down the river, a sunk spider in the roughish water (golden plover hackle and gold body preferred) does well here. These five casts make a good night's fishing from sunset to sunrise on this excellent river from end of July till October.

Whitadder.—A quarter of a mile below Hutton Bridge on the pool and stream just above Claribed Farm. Fishing off the left bank going down-stream, or fishing up from tail end of weeds, at very tail of this pool the water goes deep into left bank. This pot, about 20 feet, is real good close in for a big one. At the top of this pot you will be walking in the long grass and reeds; fish close into the rushes right up to the rough water, and when you reach the stream fish in mid-water up to the roughest bit at the neck.

Claribed Dam.—For night fishing, the top of the dam just below Claribed Farm. Cast right over the stream close to the far bank, as the best trout feed at night close to the bank here. Continue 40 yards down till the stream dies away, then come out and go in again at the broad part of river another 50 yards down— keep casting close under the trees to far bank;

continue for quite 70 yards, then go right down to the turn and fish it both sides for 25 yards. The water below this, as far as you can fish into the dam, I found only did well on a real rough night with a half gale of wind.

Above Hutton Bridge.—Start just above the arches, fishing close to steep left bank. Fishing up, good trout lie at tail end of pool, and on the hang of stream to the arches, which has a grand feeding bottom. Continue fishing up that bank till you come to overhanging tree ; this is where best fish lie—aye sure that a big one lies just under the tree. From there to head of stream, where mill lade comes in, is real good. From head of this stream miss the water at the mill until you come to the rocky bits just below Hogg's Dam, and fish behind the boulders here carefully. I knew of four trout killed in this rocky bit one afternoon in May 1917, all over $1\frac{1}{2}$ lb. each. The tail end of dam close into the boulders fishes well, then the top end in the deep pot just below the stream shelters good trout. This pot is famous for sea trout right through the back end—in fact a sea trout can be got here quite early in August, when none are found in any other part of the river.

The next stream, "The Lady Stream," is all good ; one cannot make a mistake off either bank, plenty of fish all over it when the water is not too low. During the summer of 1919 this stream was too low and never fished on account of weeds. During the early night fishing months, May and June, on a fair water at sunrise, perhaps this is the best pool on the river for a splashing rise of trout.

Jackdaw Rocks.—About half a mile below Edington Mill and one mile from Hogg's Dam always holds good trout ; tail end never found do well, but from the first 15 yards of the calm water below the stream good trout lie. Continue fishing up the rough water, casting over it within half a foot of left bank, going upstream right into the edge of the weeds. You will be surprised at the quality of trout lying in the very thin rough water here behind every big stone.

The foregoing four casts will give the reader who visits these streams a pretty good idea of where trout lie, and will apply to the majority of our small streams or waters.

I gave a description of one cast on "Tweed" above Railway Bridge, Cardrona, in Fly-fishing Chapter. When I say "four casts" it would perhaps be better to say four days' or four nights' fishing, as each one will do for an outing.

Lochs trout lie usually at all jutting-out points, behind big rocks or boulders, near clumps of weeds and, particularly when a good breeze is on, in the *broken surf* on the weather shore. The latter is usually the place the average angler misses while *loch* fishing.

To Learn Casting

Practise on a lawn at first, your line with a good knot at end. Cast at a mark, or say a piece of paper. Start with a short line, gradually lengthening till you can cast a good straight line on your object. When you think yourself proficient, try a gut cast with a fair-sized fly to light on the mark. If you practise this an hour for a day or two you will be surprised how soon you get the touch of a really good caster; make the wrist tell in casting in somewhat the same manner as one would crack a whip. That is the finish of your cast, which makes the gut line alight so gracefully on the water; through practice you will get to switch under bushes, in fact make your fly alight where you will. Then you must learn the "Speyside" cast, which is absolutely necessary when wading up a stream where bushes and trees are thick along the banks. This cast is made by drawing your line well up in front of you, then by a quick movement of the wrist making the point of the rod tell. One can throw a lovely line across any moderate sized stream. Usually a much shorter line can be used in this style of fishing if the angler does not make much movement, as he has a background behind him of trees or brushwood. It is a well-known fact that the trout cannot see the angler if he keeps still, as no part of his body is in the skyline, and no shadow ; a fairly whippy rod is necessary with this mode of fly fishing. Your line should never reach farther back than your side for the "Speyside" cast ; try it with a short line just the length of your ten-foot rod first, and gradually lengthen line till you can cover the stream.

Anglers' Weather Signs

If sheep are feeding with their backs to the wind, expect rain.

Hoar frost, sign of rain.

Trees go dark before a storm.

Tulips and dandelions close up before rain

When the leaves of trees curl with wind from south, it indicates rain.

Unusually clear atmosphere and distant objects clearly seen, means rain.

If gnats are plentiful in spring, expect a fine autumn.

If it rains before sunrise, expect a fine afternoon.

If the chaffinch often repeats its call-note " Pink," it foretells rain.

Things Worth Knowing

There is no doubt on a bright day that the flash of the gut, and perhaps the flash of the rod, are seen by the fish. To remedy this somewhat, a rod with a dull colour is by far the best to use ; also gut stained a mossy light brown or dun colour, not too dark, will be found to fish much better.

Good Rod Varnish

1 teaspoonful dark green sage paint.
35 drops amber varnish.
50 drops turpentine.
2 drops Japanese gold size.
Put on very lightly.

Gut, Dun Colour

Boil a handful of walnut tree leaves with a little soot in a quart of water. Steep the gut in the liquid until you get the desired colour.

Dye Feathers

The most difficult colour to get is olive. Dip your blae hackles or feathers in a saturated solution of picric acid boiling, or in onion juice. For all colours boil feathers in vinegar and water, then boil in aniline dyes colour required.

Colour of Ground the Colour of Fly

You will find, especially in moorland loch fishing, that a fly the same as ground colour will kill. Nature asserts itself here. Male fish usually bore to the bottom when hooked, and female fish rise and play more on the surface

Enemies to Gut

Sunlight and gas fumes are injurious, therefore keep your gut away from light when not in use, and never carry your casts on your hat, or stow away your tackle on some top shelf where the gas fumes get it.

Dibbling for Worms

Get a strong dibble, and insert it in ground, moving it back and forward. You will find the worms will come up, thinking it is their enemy the mole.

Grayling Fishing

Grayling take all the trout lures except minnow, and the hybrid of trout and grayling are the only known fish to breed.

Midge Bite

A weak solution of permanganate of potash rubbed on face and hands keeps them away.

Chaffed Heel

Wash it carefully ; mix the white of an egg with a few drops of brandy ; paint it on once or twice, and you will get an artificial skin.

Packing Fish

Never wash your trout before packing ; always pack in dry bracken leaves, next best heather, or dry wheat straw or straw of any kind.

Splinter in Hand

Can be extracted without pain by steam. Nearly fill a wide-mouthed bottle with hot water; place the injured hand over the mouth of bottle, and press lightly; the suction draws the flesh down and in a few minutes the steam will draw out the splinter.

Landing Trout

If using a net, you will often get your trout immediately after his first run, if you get his head up on surface, and slide him on top of water to the net. If you miss him, then you must play him till done. If landing ashore, draw him to side till head is just out, no more, and you can go and lift him, whereas if drawn completely out he will spring about.

Lies for Trout

One day while fishing the Whitadder with my friend B., on meeting that excellent angler Mr P. of Hutton, we sat down for a chat. P. made the remark, pointing to a big stone in the pool below us, that if one could prove it he would bet all he possessed there was a big trout behind that stone, as many the good trout he had killed there. Shortly after, on rising, P. said, "Creep both of you cautiously in line behind me." On looking over, we found a shaft of light had struck over the side of the stone showing the bed of the river, and there, sure enough, to our surprise were five trout lying in line behind the stone. The first trout would be a good pounder, and the other four from threequarters to four ounces.

Greenwell's Glory

This fly is undoubtedly the best all-round trout fly ever dressed. It imitates so many of the natural flies that one cannot make a mistake fishing it all the season. It might not be out of place here to give the history of the fly, and how it came to be so named, given to the writer by the late Mr James Wright of Sprouston, who was the first to dress it. Canon Greenwell, while fishing the Tweed one day, observed that the trout were rising to another fly besides the March brown then on the water. Catching some of them, he brought them up to Mr Wright to dress an imitation. They agreed that the hen blackbird wing with black red hackles tied with yellow silk waxed and gold twist was the correct dressing. The

Canon, during that day and the day following, killed a big basket with them. Mr Wright proposed that the new fly be named, and for that night arranged a meeting. Mr Robert Wright (who was then courting his future wife, Miss Brown, the schoolmaster's daughter), while visiting asked the dominie to come to the meeting. There were present Canon Greenwell, Mr and Mrs James Wright, Messrs Robert Wright, Brown, Thomas Kerss and his two sons Charles and James, Plumber Johnstone, with several angling gentlemen from Durham, who were staying at the Club House. The dominie was in the chair. Mr James Wright proposed they call the fly "Greenwell's Glory," and so it was christened, and that name will live as long as there are trout to catch.

The Rod

If you have overcome the rudiments of casting, and can throw a fair line, the best rod you can use for fly fishing is 10 to $10\frac{1}{2}$ feet, two pieces spliced preferred, otherwise two or three pieces weighing about nine ounces; a point that yields to least touch; and make sure there is no stiffness at any one joint, but a gentle swing from butt to point; green-

heart, with lancewood top or top with whale-
bone tip with an agate tip ring, snake rings to
balance the rod. Such a rod one can fish a
whole day without tiring, and if the angler is
at all expert can kill fish up to 6 lb. weight
with ease. I have fished what I consider the
most perfect trout rod, " Anderson's Dunkeld "
$8\frac{1}{2}$ ounces, for over twenty years, and killed
sea trout up to $8\frac{1}{2}$ lb. with it. After eighteen
years' fishing I had one new top-piece to buy.
This rod is as straight to-day as the day it
was bought. To show how well balanced a rod
is to be perfect, the writer once put a new agate
top ring on the " Dunkeld " and could not
understand the extraordinary change that had
come over it, as it did not fish half so well as
previously. On taking the rod to my old friend,
Mr Anderson, he at once pointed out that the
new tip ring had completely altered the balance.
He further surprised me by stating that so well
balanced was a good trout rod that he has
known the sand-papering and revarnishing of a
rod spoil it . from such an authority the reader
can rely the statement is correct

The Reel

Should at all times balance the rod. The all-brass reels are now of the past, as aluminium and vulcanite have taken their place. Then you can get strength and lightness combined. Never buy a riveted reel, because if you get sand in the drum it is almost impossible to get it cleaned : so see that your reel is screwed, and thus easily taken to pieces. Make sure of a free, running reel, which is the secret of being able to use a light rod and fine tackle.

The Line

Endless variety, too numerous to mention ; the finest waterproof lines being sold are quite good enough to land anything up to 10 lb., with 50 yards and a free-running reel.

Particular care should be taken every time you return from fishing to dry your line well. If you have not got a line-drier, the backs of two chairs will do. Make a practice of doing this, and your line will last ten times as long as one left on fishing-reel till the next outing.

Waders

To those who can use fishing waders without going over the top every outing (as the writer invariably did with creeping and crawling), they are best—first, because in trout fishing one very seldom need wade over the knee, and secondly, because they are healthier than fishing trousers. The great advantage of the latter is that one can sit down anywhere, and for night fishing are much warmer. Let the trousers be very wide at the top to let in as much air as possible. As one who values health and comfort, the writer has proved it is false economy continually patching waders. Once they begin to go in one or two places, it is far cheaper in the long run to buy a new pair. One day's wetting may cost you a doctor's bill the price of three pairs.

Brogues

The general opinion among anglers is that shoes are neither comfortable nor thrifty for wading. A good strong pair of leather or canvas boots well shod with large tackets, though heavy, are comfortable in the water, and you are less liable to slip and get sprained ankles.

Landing Net

Medium size, say 18 inches, with 3-foot handle, and if carried on basket, thus—

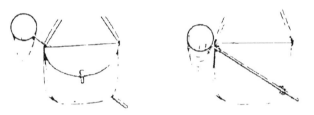

Two leather rings or straps tied on back of basket, one at top right-hand corner, the other at bottom left-hand corner.   The net is out of the way and easily got at when required.

Clothing

All I can advise about clothing is, don't wear anything black; heather-coloured green mixture suit is best.

There may be nothing really novel in my theories and ideas on angling.   I know I am courting criticism from hosts of anglers regarding some of my ideas, more especially those on loch fishing. All I can say is, they are the personal experiences of the lifetime of a practical angler. There may be many faults in the manner in which I have tried to explain how to get trout, but one thing is sure, if properly applied they do catch them.

A great many anglers fish for many years and never seem to get any further forward in the art than, say, after their first six months This is through lack of observation of the habits of the trout, and through never looking to the expert for advice. The angler should learn more of the habits of trout every time he goes to the water. After a time, quite unconsciously, he will find he has developed the instinct to tell exactly where trout will be lying. Once the angler reaches this stage, the art never becomes wearisome. Angling is most conducive to health and mental peacefulness. A keen angler forgets all worries, business or otherwise, when plying the gentle art, therefore it is the best of all sports as a complete rest to the busy man. For even during winter you can pass a pleasing time thinking over one of the grand days you have had, and having the water in your mind's eye.

All keen anglers are passionate lovers of Nature. Many an angler will tell you he has had a real good day though the creel is almost empty, because he has enjoyed Nature at its best by the banks of the stream.

PRINTED BY OLIVER AND BOYD EDINBURGH